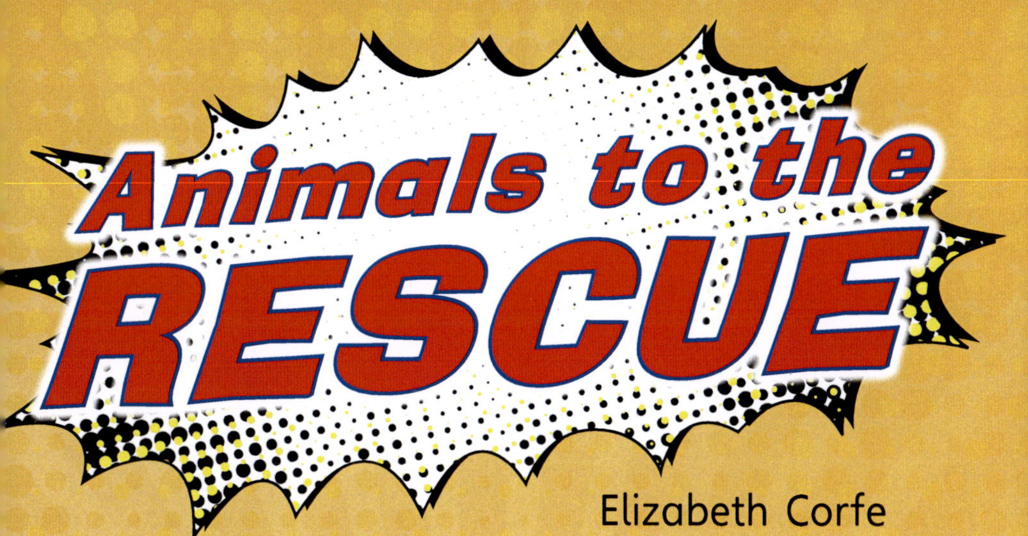

Elizabeth Corfe

Contents

Animals SAVE LIVES

Imagine if you were lost outside in the freezing cold, in the middle of winter… what animal do you think would save you?

If you said a dog, especially one who loves smelly socks, you would be right!

Dogs and other animals of all shapes and sizes save lives everyday.

Clever PIGEONS

Pigeons are found all over the world but there is more to these birds than you think. One pigeon was so brave, he became a hero!

Cher Ami – The Pigeon Hero

In World War I, in France, nearly 200 American soldiers were trapped near the **enemy** and needed to be rescued. Their army didn't know their soldiers were in danger and were dropping bombs right on top of them.

an Amercian fighter plane dropping bombs

A trained army pigeon called Cher Ami came to the soldiers' rescue. A soldier attached a note to the pigeon's leg, and Cher Ami flew home to the **army base**, about 40 kilometres away.

While Cher Ami was flying home, the enemy shot his leg but he kept going. The brave pigeon delivered the note in 25 minutes! Thanks to Cher Ami, the bombing stopped and the soldiers were rescued.

The note Cher Ami delivered told the American army where the soldiers were, and asked them to "please stop dropping bombs on us!"

Cher Ami: the Facts

Name:	*Cher Ami* is French for "Dear Friend".
Who:	An American army carrier pigeon
When and Where:	World War I, France
What:	Cher Ami helped save nearly 200 soldiers.

Cher Ami became a hero, and was given a special medal for his bravery.

Homing Pigeons

Cher Ami was a homing pigeon. Homing pigeons are birds that have been bred and trained to always find their way home. As long as they know where their home is, they will always find it!

Dogs and THEIR JOBS

Dogs are more than our best friends. Some dogs find missing people, act as crime detectives and work as special helpers.

Search and Rescue Dogs

Some of the world's best search and rescue workers aren't paid with money. They're paid with smelly socks! Read on to find out why.

Search and rescue dogs help in disasters, such as earthquakes. These clever **canines** use their noses to sniff for missing or trapped people.

This search and rescue dog is looking for trapped people after an earthquake.

The Asian Tsunami

In 2004, a huge **tsunami** (say: *soo-nah-mee*) hit parts of Asia. Homes were destroyed, and many people lost their lives.

The enormous waves from the tsunami destroyed buildings.

Lots of people were trapped under fallen buildings, homes and trees. Rescue workers could not find them all and needed help. Enter the search and rescue dogs! These dogs found many people who were trapped. Read on to find out how!

How do search and rescue dogs find people?

Search and rescue dogs are trained to use their **senses** – mainly their sense of smell. When the dogs keep sniffing in the one spot, rescue workers know someone might be trapped nearby. The dog has done its job.

Just like your dog at home, search and rescue dogs love **rewards**. These dogs get big 'thank you' pats, and sometimes get to play a game of tug-of-war with an old, smelly sock! Ewww!

Detective Dogs

Other dogs use their great sense of smell for a different type of job. These dogs can sniff out bombs, guns and even food, using their noses. That's why you see sniffer dogs at airports – they sniff people's bags!

Detective dogs are also called "sniffer dogs".

Why food?!

Sniffer dogs sniff for food because fruit, vegetables and meat can carry insects. Some insects can **invade** an environment and cause a lot of harm. When you travel, you cannot take some foods into some countries.

Service Dogs

Other dogs help people live their lives more easily. These dogs are called service dogs. They help people with **disabilities**.

Service dogs need to have a good **temperament**, good health, and be smart and strong.

Service dogs help people around the house, at work, at school or just out and about. They can help people do everyday things such as crossing the road and closing a door. They also give friendship and love to their owners.

These special service dogs can:

- close doors
- pick up things
- turn lights on and off
- bark for help
- get the phone

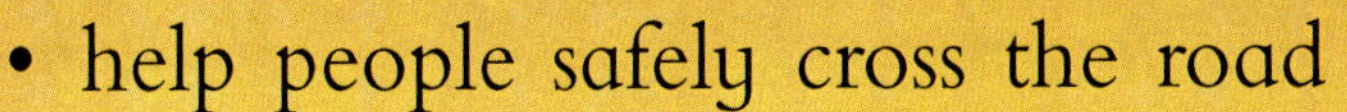

- help people safely cross the road
- get bottles of water from the fridge
- pull wheelchairs.

This service dog is pushing a buzzer to help its owner open a door.

This service dog is helping its owner shop at the supermarket. It has picked up the cat food!

Smart, SUPER HEROES

Smart Sniffers

Rats are very smart animals. Rats help to save people that live in places **affected** by war.

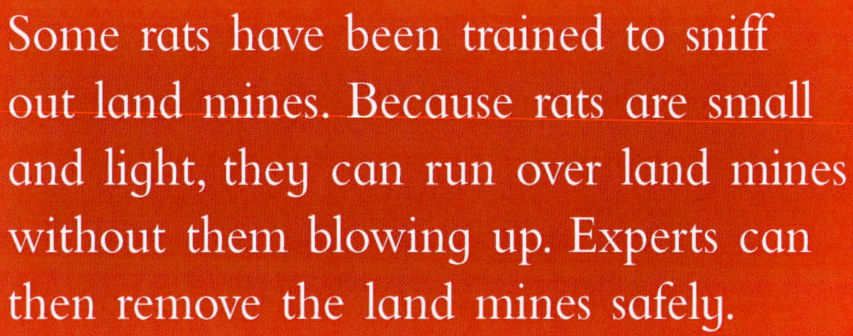

Some rats have been trained to sniff out land mines. Because rats are small and light, they can run over land mines without them blowing up. Experts can then remove the land mines safely.

It takes between six months to one year to train a rat to sniff out land mines.

A rat's sense of smell works just as well as a dog's. When a rat sniffs out a land mine, they sit and scratch at the spot until they are rewarded with food.

Doctor Dracula

Leeches are slimy creatures that suck blood.

Leeches have been used in medicine for thousands of years. Today, doctors still use leeches on patients. They can heal sore skin and help pump blood to damaged body parts.

This is the rear sucker of a leech used in a hospital.

Leeches can suck your blood for six hours!

Leeches heal by injecting some saliva when they suck blood. This saliva has a **chemical** in it which helps blood flow and brings **oxygen** to help the wound heal.

Super Sonar Soldiers

These soldiers are not your normal soldiers – they have flippers and fins! Navy dolphins are used to find missing navy divers, find lost things, and even find underwater bombs!

How do they find the bombs?

All dolphins find things using sounds and echoes, or **sonar**. Navy dolphins use sonar to find the underwater bombs, and drop floating markers above them. This tells navy divers where the bomb is.

This dolphin is searching for an underwater bomb. When it finds the bomb, it will place the yellow marker on it. Then, the bomb will be removed safely.

Whales and bats use sonar to find food and to help them find their way.

What Do YOU THINK?

Having **specially** trained animals to help people is a good thing. But what about the animals put in dangerous environments, such as those trained to find bombs?

Do you think this is the right thing to do?

Animals help people in many ways. They even risk their own lives to save ours. So let's make sure we look after all our special, brave and amazing friends. You never know, one day you may need an animal to help rescue you!

1. Cher Ami was:
   - **a** a search and rescue dog
   - **b** a carrier pigeon
   - **c** a dolphin
2. As a reward, search and rescue dogs may get to play with:
   - **a** a tennis ball
   - **b** an old bone
   - **c** a smelly sock
3. Leeches can suck blood for up to:
   - **a** 24 hours
   - **b** 2 days
   - **c** 6 hours
4. To find underwater bombs dolphins use:
   - **a** underwater cameras
   - **b** sonar
   - **c** their sense of smell

Answers

1. b a carrier pigeon
2. c a smelly sock
3. c 6 hours
4. b sonar

affected	changed by something
army base	a place where soldiers work and where equipment is located
canines	dogs
chemical	a substance
disabilities	a lack or loss of the ability to do things that most people can do
enemy	a person or group that wants to hurt or fight another group
invade	to enter as an enemy
oxygen	a gas breathed by humans and animals
rewards	things given in return for good work or helping someone
senses	sight, hearing, smell, taste or touch – things that make us aware of what is around us
sonar	a system using echoes from underwater soundwaves to find the position of things
specially	for a particular purpose
temperament	the personality and feelings of a person or animal
tsunami	a huge wave caused by an earthquake under the ocean

Index